T0065237

HOW TO WIN CUSTODY

HOW TO WIN CUSTODY

BRIAN D. PERSKIN, ESQ.

HOW TO WIN CUSTODY

iUniverse books may be ordered through booksellers or by contacting:

iUniverse
1663 Liberty Drive
Bloomington, IN 47403
www.iuniverse.com
844-349-9409

Because of the dynamic nature of the Internet, any web addresses or links contained in this book may have changed since publication and may no longer be valid. The views expressed in this work are solely those of the author and do not necessarily reflect the views of the publisher, and the publisher hereby disclaims any responsibility for them.

Any people depicted in stock imagery provided by Getty Images are models, and such images are being used for illustrative purposes only.
Certain stock imagery © Getty Images.

ISBN: 978-1-6632-1404-1 (sc)
ISBN: 978-1-6632-1405-8 (e)

Library of Congress Control Number: 2020923854

Print information available on the last page.

iUniverse rev. date: 11/25/2020

Intelligent and Aggressive Representation for Every Person Going Through Divorce or Custody Proceedings in the State of New York
You can call me any time on 718 875-7584
Reach me via email: bdp@perskinlaw.com
Visit my website: www.newyorkdivorceattorney.com
Schedule a consultation: https://live.vcita.com/site/brianperskin

A lawyer's job is to create a better strategy than the one you have, or the one that you just have not yet thought of. My firm's strategy in every case is to evaluate the law and the facts and design a conscious and deliberate process specifically for you. It is our belief that our process will ensure future, success in your case.

CONTENTS

INTRODUCTION

Finalizing a divorce is a stressful process; when combined with a child custody battle it only adds to the weight of that difficult situation. There are so many factors taken into consideration during a custody battle, and the more you are prepared before starting the process the better you will be able to present your case.

Winning child custody ultimately comes down to you being happy with the outcome of your custody situation, and that arrangements have been made in the best interests of your child. This ideal outcome is will differ depending on each situation. You may feel it is best for you to get sole custody of your child, or maybe it is in the best interests of your family to share joint custody. Every custody hearing is unique, and the outcome is completely dependent on your specific family circumstances. Because of this, it is can be very beneficial to work with experienced professionals to ensure you have the best chance at receiving the outcome you believe is best for your specific situation.

In order to have the best chance at winning your child custody battle, you need to have a clear parenting plan in place to present to the Judge. You will need to work with both an attorney as well as a psychologist to build and prove your case.

This guide will walk you through the necessary steps to ensure you are as prepared as possible so you will have the best chance for success.

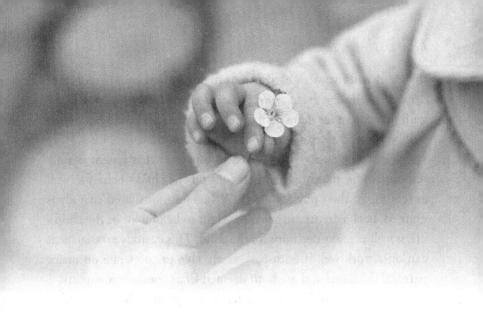

PREPARATION

CUSTODY TYPES

Custody is a term used to describe the legal and practical relationship between parents and their children. It defines the legal right of the parent(s) to be able to make decisions for the children, as well as their obligation to care for the child.

There are few different outcomes that are possible when it comes to custody arrangements, and two main types - **Legal Custody**, and **Physical Custody.** Whichever parent is granted Legal Custody has the right to make important decisions about a child's care including, but not limited to, medical care and religious upbringing. If the parents are given joint legal custody, the parents will make those decisions together, regardless of which parent the child is living with.

Whichever parent is granted Physical Custody, or residential custody, will be responsible for the actual care and supervision of the child. If the Judge decides that *joint physical custody* is warranted, the child will live with each parent divided in an equal amount of time. If the Judge grants **sole physical custody**, the child will live with that parent for more than 50% of the time, and the other parent will be allowed a certain amount of visitation time.

When sole custody is granted to a parent, that parent is fully responsible for making legal decisions on the child's behalf as well as tending to their physical needs. When joint or shared custody is granted, both parents are given the right to be present in the child's life as well as make decisions for the child. This custody arrangement can only work well if both parents are able to cooperate on major parental decisions and are both deemed fit as competent parents.

The term custodial parent refers to the parent who has primary physical custody of his or her child. The custodial parent resides with the child for the majority of the time and has the most responsibility for the child even if there is a joint custody arrangement and the other parent plays a very active role in the child's life. The non-custodial parent is the parent who does not have physical custody of his or her child. It is possible, however, for a non-custodial parent to have legal custody, or the authority to make decisions about the child. They also may have visitation rights and be highly involved in their child's life.

The court makes decisions regarding child custody based on what they deem is in the best interests of the child. In order to decide what these best interest are, the court examines factors including (but not limited to):

- Who the primary caretaker of the child is
- The child's wishes
- The physical and mental health of each parent and the child
- The parenting abilities of each parent
- Each party's work schedule and childcare plan
- The child's relationship with each parent
- Any incidences of domestic violence or child abuse

- Where the child resides when the custody application is being reviewed
- The parents' willingness to communicate with each other, etc.

You should aim to build a support system of knowledgeable and dependable people to surround yourself with as you go through this process. Never underestimate the power that good advice can have when it comes to winning your case.

LOGIC & COMMITMENT

There are several things you should do when preparing your case, to ensure you have the best possible chance of having your desired outcome. There are also some things you should avoid when possible.

If there is ever a time to use logic over emotion, it is during a child custody battle. Many parents make the grave mistake of acting out of emotion when fighting for custody of their child, for two main reasons. First, anything pertaining to your child's safety and well-being, is an emotional subject. Secondly, there is often unresolved anger or discord between you and your partner, so your ability to cope with those issues may diminish more and more as time goes on.

In order to have the best chance at winning your case, you **must** be able to think clearly and concisely, and most importantly, control your emotions. Allowing your emotions to take over will diminish your credibility. If you operate from a place of anger or animosity, it will affect your ability to present your case effectively, and it will also affect the way you appear to the Judge. Operating from a place of fear or doubt isn't helpful either, as you will likely get shut down by your partner due to lack of drive. You need to exhibit courage, to stand up for yourself and for your child. You don't need to lock all your emotions away, and not feel anything. You need to make sure you are projecting them in the best possible way.

If you find yourself having a particularly hard time managing your emotions, it might be beneficial to seek counseling during this process. Then, you can work through any emotional issues you are facing with a trained professional, who will help to give you some coping skills. Then you will be able to execute your plan in the most effective way.

There is likely a certain amount of conflict between you and your partner, and unfortunately the custody process usually exacerbates this. When you actively operate from a place of logic rather than emotion, you will convey information better, and in turn, respond more appropriately to whatever situations arise. You should approach the custody battle as you would approach a business decision. First, set a clear goal (or goals) and then determine the steps you need to take to ensure you reach that outcome. Being in control of your emotions will give you the best chance of dealing with any obstacles you may encounter as you fight this battle. Remember, the stakes of this battle are directly related to the wellbeing of your children.

Keeping your emotions at bay is something you need to practice for the duration of the process. Commitment to your case is also **absolutely vital** to achieving the outcome you desire. You are likely to encounter unexpected circumstances during the custody process, and you need to be able to stay focused and determined, regardless of the obstacles you may face.

While you may think you know your partner very well, you never know what lengths someone will go to when it comes to fighting for the rights to obtain custody of their child. You need to be prepared to adjust your strategy as you proceed, because you can never know exactly how external factors are going affect your case. Unfortunately, your ideal outcome is not guaranteed, but the amount you prepare and the way you present your evidence will greatly affect the conclusion of your case. There are two things you have complete control of, and they are your own preparedness and the way you react to anything or anyone trying to throw you off course.

BIRD'S NEST CO-PARENTING

Most child custody cases begin with divorce, and divorce can bring out the worst in people. If the parents cannot settle an agreement through mediation, a child custody case will be decided in a court of law. In a perfect world, you would be able to co-parent peacefully with your partner. There is even a method that is growing in popularity called **Bird's Nest Co-Parenting**, which is when the children remain living under one roof while their divorced parents move between homes.

There are pros and cons to this method, which are as follows:

Pros:

- It can create a sense of normalcy for children which can be good for their well-being
- Allows children to remain close to their friends and in the same school
- Prevents parents from having to sell the marital home quickly

Cons:

- May be more difficult for parents to cope with their divorce
- Can lead to arguments between parents about bills and utilities
- There is a possibility that bird's nest co-parenting may be too costly for each parent
- Lack of privacy and the possibility of tension once new significant others are introduced to the child

While joint custody and some variation of co-parenting are typically preferable outcomes, they are only an effective option if both parents are able to act amicably towards each other.

It may be in your best interests to anticipate the worst from your partner when it comes to fighting for the rights of your child. It is always better to be over-prepared than to underestimate the lengths your partner will go to in order to convince the Judge that they are the more suitable parent.

This is one of the many reasons why it is imperative for you to be open and honest about everything when presenting your case. Know your strengths and weaknesses and try to evaluate what your partner's strengths and weakness are. This can help when formulating your plan of action. Depending on your situation, it may be helpful to keep audio or video records of any interactions you have with your partner throughout the process, or at least have a reliable witness present. This is especially important when you have any interactions where your child or children will be present. If you are effectively managing your emotions and you partner is not, it is crucial to have that information on record.

It is also important to show that you have put in some time and effort into understanding your state custody laws. Not only will this help you in feeling confident in your knowledge of how the process works, it will show that you are committed to the case and have your child's wellbeing as a top priority.

GOALS VS. OUTCOME

Regardless of the relationship you currently have with your partner, you need to show that you are open and willing to do anything and everything that needs to be done, to keep the case moving efficiently and effectively. Your case will be much better received if you appear cooperative and sincere rather than aggressive or combative.

Be prepared to remain actively involved in your case from start to finish. Plan ahead, keep your focus on your goals, but also allow yourself to be adaptable to whatever unknown roadblocks you may encounter. You may have a strong opinion on how the case should be determined, but a psychologist and Judge may take factors into consideration that you have not.

Depending on the age of your child, it may be helpful for you to talk with them about their wants and expectations. Keeping an open line of communication is essential to understanding how your child is processing the situation. This doesn't mean planting false information in their minds about your spouse, or oversharing details that may stress or concern them. Simply being a source of constant support for your child throughout this difficult process is very important.

As mentioned, every single child custody case is unique, so it can be very hard to discern what the outcome will be. The best thing you can do is prepare detailed and accurate evidence to support your case. Ultimately, it is up to the Judge and the psychologist in the case who will determine what is best for your child, based on all of the evidence they have available to them.

No matter how thoroughly a case is reviewed or how much attention is given to the divorce, there is always the possibility that the custody agreement will not be sufficient to remain effective for months or years after the case has been finalized. In some states, you can modify a child custody order if there has been a significant change in circumstances since the outcome was determined. If that is something you encounter, you can file a modification petition with the help of an experienced family lawyer. The court will apply the same principles as done in the original case to determining a new custody arrangement.

As with the original formation of a custody agreement, the courts will always judge modifications in light of what is best for the child or children involved. Therefore, modifications to custody agreements are generally approved when it can be proven that the change will be for the betterment of the child or children. It must be proven that a substantial change in circumstance has occurred, which now requires an analysis of the previously determined terms and conditions.

Substantial changes could include a geographic move or a change in lifestyle such as a new job or development of drug or alcohol abuse problem. These are circumstances that will need to be brought before the court and substantially proven in order to obtain the modification. As such, these are also circumstances that will require the additional support and guidance of qualified attorney.

When a child custody case is brought to the court, the court will try to accommodate the best interest of the child as well as the environment that offers the most stability. Some of the other factors that will be taken into consideration when deciding on the outcome of a child custody battle are:

- The child's age, gender, mental and physical health
- The parent's mental and physical health
- The parent's lifestyle
- Any history of child abuse
- The emotional bond between the parent and child
- The parent's ability to provide the child with food, shelter, clothing, and medical care
- The child's regular routine
- The quality of the child's education
- The child's preference, if the child is above a certain age (this is usually around age 12)
- The ability and willingness of the parent to encourage communication and contact between the child and the other parent

The court may also conduct a Child Custody Evaluation. An evaluation usually consists of interviews, psychological exams, and analysis of the children, and perhaps the parents. However, the court has the ability to deny a parent's request for an evaluation. The Child Custody Evaluation process will be discussed later on in this book.

CUSTODY EVALUTION

Whether you are the one who requested a custody evaluation or have been informed that you need to meet with a child custody evaluator, it is important to be prepared for such an important process. Here are some helpful tips from our custody attorneys regarding how best prepare a custody evaluation:

- **Respect the Custody Evaluator** – He or she is an independent contractor and is meant to be impartial. They are not your friend, nor are they your enemy. Treat them with respect at all times in order to protect your character and the possible outcome of your evaluation.

- **Prepare for the Custody Evaluation** – it is important to show the evaluator that you are prepared. Have your documents and your answers prepared in advance so that the evaluator sees you as responsible, as well as respectful of their time.

- **Prepare Documentation** – The more documentation you have prepared in advance, the smoother the process will be. Provide records of any and all time spent with your child such as school schedules, after school activities and transportation, doctor's appointments, etc. These can help prove the type of family dynamic you have and the relationship you work hard to maintain with your child.

- **Keep Your Home in Readiness** – Home visits show an evaluator the type of home environment you provide to your child. Keep your home clean and organized, especially for the home visit, to put your best face forward.

- **Control Your Emotions** – Custody evaluations and home visits can be stressful and you are responsible for how you respond to these situations. The way you act during the evaluation can affect the outcome. Keep this in mind and stay in control of your emotions at all times.

QUESTIONS TO CONSIDER

Most parents want their child in their life in some way, but it is important to analyze what is in the best interest of that child. There are many factors to consider, including the following:

- Are you the best parent to raise your child?
- If so, is it in the best interest of your child for you to raise them on your own?
- Are you able to reach an amicable settlement outside of court?
- Do you have enough evidence to win your case?
- If not, what steps can you take to ensure you attain the necessary evidence?
- Do you have the financial ability to sue for custody?
- How much damage will your child endure emotionally from you suing for custody?
- How much damage will your child endure emotionally if you *don't* sue for custody?
- What are your strengths and weaknesses when it comes to parenting?
- What are your spouse's strengths and weakness when it comes to parenting?
- What outcome is in the best interests for your child?

Often times, a certain amount of compromise will result in the best outcome for your family. There is so much information to take into consideration when it comes to finalizing where a child is going to grow and develop. This process should not be taken lightly. It will take a lot of time and effort, and it will likely take a toll on your emotional well-being. When it comes to the welfare of your children, you have to be willing and prepared to do everything it takes to ensure their needs are being met.

COMMON ROADBLOCKS

HANDLING DISHONESTY

Dishonesty is something you may encounter in the process of your custody battle. Inside a courtroom, even when sworn in before testifying, people perjure themselves constantly. There are limitless reasons why people may do this, and some reasons include:

- They think that it is necessary in order to protect their children, or to protect themselves
- To improve their chances of winning
- To alienate the other parent from the child
- To hide an affair or inappropriate behavior
- To hide their sexual orientation
- To hide money, other assets or substance abuse issues
- They may not have enough money to pay for an attorney to represent them

Whatever the reason may be, lying should be avoided at all costs during your trial. Honesty is always the better option, and will save you a world of potential problems that would occur if you got caught in a lie. Lying is not only wrong, it can and has reversed custody. One reason being, psychologists believe that a parent who is willing to lie is more likely to teach their children to lie. In some cases, if a parent is a pathological liar, it could be evidence of a personality disorder. Proving enough dishonesty in your spouse could lead to a diagnosis by a psychologist. Pathological lying entails a deep-seated manipulation that is not only morally wrong, but is detrimental to raising children. On top of that, it will only cause more issues and confrontation in the future.

There are certain steps you can and should take to catch your partner if they are choosing to be dishonest. One of the most important tools to have, is a detailed and consistent journal. This can help your case in a variety of ways. It can identify issues, personalities, witnesses and keep a record of any evidence you are building for your case. Furthermore, a journal can be the foundation of your case, and it is something you should start creating immediately. It will help to develop a chronology of yours and your partners behaviors and actions. Proving dishonesty does not ensure an automatic win, but it does help to support you and your case. The more honest and accurate evidence you can use to your advantage, the better.

There are certain investigative techniques you can use to help catch your partner in a lie. Whenever possible, try to have a third-party witness who can attest to the evidence you collect when doing this. As mentioned previously, try to record any interactions with your partner using audio or video recordings. Keep track of any records that could be beneficial to your case, including those audio/video files, and any police reports if applicable. You do not need to be aggressive when doing this or try to instigate certain behaviors from your spouse. Simply collecting consistent, detailed evidence against your spouse surrounding any and all important issues will help you to build a solid case.

Attorneys can also uncover lies through a deposition, which is a sworn testimony prior to going to court. Information collected during a deposition can be a very valuable asset to your case. If you have any reason to believe your spouse may be dishonest, make sure you discuss this with your attorney prior to the deposition so they are as prepared as possible and ask the right questions. Your attorney should have a printed copy of all evaluations in their possession months before going to trial; make sure you examine it closely to highlight anything that seems suspicious. You can then add that information to the collection of evidence you gather when building your case.

VISITATION EXCHANGES

Depending on the relationship you have with your spouse, a visitation exchange can be a tumultuous situation. If you have any reason to believe this may be the case for you, it is even more important to bring an unbiased witness with you. If warranted, you could even take a private investigator or an off-duty police officer with you. This is especially important if you think there is a chance that your partner may become violent or attempt to call the police themselves. This is also the perfect example of a time and place where you should be ready to keep a video and/or audio record.

Awareness is key when it comes to anticipating behaviors in a custody exchange. Custody exchanges could prove that your partner is confrontational or vindictive, which is a perfect example of the kind of event you should be recording in your journal. Make sure you arrive early so you can scope out the situation and see if you can predict any conflict that may arise. Sometimes a parent will attempt to trap the other parent by claiming harassment during a visitation exchange, and they may even file a restraining order. This should only be done if it is truly warranted because if it is later proved that it wasn't, it can greatly harm your case. On the other hand, if you request a restraining order and the Judge deems that it was the appropriate course of action, that can earn you credibility within your case.

Visitation exchanges always occur with your child or children present, so be extremely aware of your own behavior during this time. This interaction is not the time to fight with your spouse; it is a time to put on a happy face to ensure you are not giving your spouse any ammunition to use against you. Make the visitation exchange as seamless as possible for your child's sake. At the same time, remember that you can never predict how your spouse is going to act during the exchange so try to remain calm and collected, but ready to act if anything unexpected should occur. Communicate as openly and effectively as you can when it comes to setting the dates and times of the visitation exchange. Keep records in your journals of this information, and if needed, record any calls or communication issues that occur, like if your partner cancels last minute, or isn't where they are scheduled to be. A parent may purposely give their partner inaccurate timing or location information, in an attempt to make it seem as though you have not followed the agreed upon instructions. If you encounter this and are able to prove it, you can use it to your advantage. It will show that your partner is being deceptive and manipulative in trying to set up a trap for you.

While setting up a trap may not seem like something you want to do, sometimes it is necessary. If your spouse has specific negative patterns and behaviors that you know to be unhealthy for your child, but has the ability to manipulate others into not seeing that, it can help your case to find ways to prove these actions. A visitation exchange may best highlight this and collecting that kind of evidence can be vital in supporting your case.

PARENTAL ALIENATION SYNDROME

A common occurrence during divorce and custody battles is one parent attempting to alienate the child from the other parent. This is often done in an attempt to retain full custody or limit the visitation rights of the other parent. Whether in the case of sole or joint custody, a parent will use their position of trust and the power over the relationship with their child to brainwash or program the child. They can make the child believe that the other parent does not love them, that the divorce was their fault or otherwise convince the child that he or she does not want to see the other parent. This can result in Parental Alienation Syndrome (PAS) and it is a recognized disorder. Some of the signs of this disorder you may see in your child include:

- Your relationship with your child has started deteriorating
- Your child no longer wants to visit you, for no apparent reason
- Your child has started to blame you for the divorce
- Your child has begun using mature words or phrasing to explain why they don't want to visit or why you are to blame (this is done when they are fed these words by the other parent)

Parental Alienation is often committed in underhanded and secret ways. By working closely with your lawyer, they can help to provide you with options in order to prove it has happened and start working toward ensuring it does not continue. Your lawyer will help you understand the signs to look for as a preventative measure and can help you take legal action against your spouse if this is already occurring. This is another reason why you should always ensure there is an open line of communication with your child.

MISCONDUCT & ABUSE

Facing allegations of child abuse or neglect can be highly nerve-racking and upsetting for parents. Child Protective Service investigations can have serious legal consequences, including a potential loss of custody or an infringement upon your parental rights. If you are facing allegations of child abuse or neglect, it is important to consult with a <u>family law attorney</u> to obtain information about your rights and develop a plan of action to deal with the allegations. An <u>experienced attorney</u> can assist you with any investigation or proceeding involving Child Protective Services, and can advise you on what to do and what to avoid in order to safeguard the interests of you and your family.

When allegations of child abuse, neglect, or endangerment are made, the state can intervene if the parents in question are considered unfit to adequately care for their children. In certain states, there are offices that investigate allegations of child abuse and neglect, aiming to protect the well-being of youth. However, parents retain the right to challenge allegations of abuse against them. An attorney can help you protect your parental rights and challenge a report of abuse or neglect made against you.

When a parent has a history of domestic violence, this can drastically affect the outcome of custody or visitation agreements. When a Judge determines custody and visitation agreements, they will do so only after careful evaluation of all factors, including any history of abuse or violent crimes for either parent. If you have been wrongfully accused of violence towards your spouse or children, it is important to gather as much evidence as possible to show that this was untrue.

Since the Judge must make a decision that is in the best interests of the child, the Judge may not grant custody, partial custody or even visitation to a parent accused or convicted of a domestic violence offense. Victims or alleged victims of domestic violence can file for Orders of Protection which can prevent a parent from coming into contact with their child.

Investigating and proving abuse can be crucial to building your case; if a psychologist determines that your spouse has inflicted abuse on your child, not only will it help you in building your case against them, the psychologist can notify any authorities if necessary to ensure the child avoids any future abuse. Most importantly, you will be able to get the child out of that unsafe environment and into more suitable living conditions.

The common types of abuse and their corresponding indicators will be described in detail within a further chapter. Remember, **it is extremely important to document all evidence that supports your suspicions about your spouse being abusive,** prior to and during this entire process.

PARENTAL KIDNAPPING

In extreme cases, one parent may take or retain the child from the other. This is called Parental Kidnapping, and it is one of the most traumatic events that anyone can endure. If your child is kidnapped by your spouse, you will need to involve every agency available to you, including law enforcement, childcare workers, schools, neighbors and employers. Interview as many people as possible, because any information you gather can help to return your child to safety.

There are many laws currently in place that can help you to recover your child, including the Uniform Child Custody Jurisdiction Act. This act was formed to avoid any potential controversy that can occur over what state has power to decide the outcome of a jurisdictional conflict, which is extremely helpful if your spouse has taken your child outside of the state. If a child abduction has occurred, the parent responsible has grossly violated the law, and there are some steps you should take, including:

- Hiring a private investigator
- Hiring an attorney if you don't already have one
- Reporting the abduction to the police
- Reporting the abduction to the FBI
- Reporting the abduction to the National Center for Missing & Exploited Children

A qualified attorney can help you navigate through the legality of this issue. Your local police officers and other law enforcement will assist you in locating your child. Stay vigilant, because many times a parental kidnapping will be preceded by a few things, including visitational interference or parental alienation. If this happens, be sure to document this process because it will help in building a case against your spouse.

ATTORNEYS

HOW TO CHOOSE A LAWYER

<u>A qualified attorney</u> is critical to building and winning your case, so it is very important to practice due diligence when deciding which lawyer you want to add to your support system. A good place to start is <u>finding a law firm that specializes in child custody cases</u>. You can check your state bar (which is a membership of attorneys licensed to practice law in your state) where there will be a list of lawyers who are rated and have certification for specializations. There are some lawyers who specialize in domestic relations or family law and they will know the best way in which to build and present your evidence to the Judge.

It is also important to try and find a lawyer who you feel comfortable communicating with. Some attorneys have a 'bedside manner' similar to doctors and can come across as 'standoff-ish' while others can be attentive and engaging. This is an emotional process, so you need to feel comfortable confiding in your lawyer. It is imperative that you are able to communicate effectively with your attorney to ensure you have the best chance at building a solid case. They will be helping you work through a lengthy and important process, so you need to feel comfortable working with them.

Hiring an attorney can be costly, but the price will be well worth it in the end. They have extensive experience and knowledge that are invaluable to your case. Some tips for keeping your costs down are faxing any updates as they occur and supporting your case with information you build on your own and from friends, family and neighbors. The success of your case does not fall solely on your lawyer, but providing them with open and honest information will help to ensure the best possible outcome.

QUESTIONS TO ASK

Choosing a lawyer should not be a snap decision; always do thorough research when determining who you want to add to your support system. Here are some examples of questions to ask when speaking with potential attorneys:

- What experience do you have with child custody cases?
- What percentage of your caseload is dedicated to handling child custody cases?
- How long have you been in practice?
- What is your track record of success?
- Do you have any special skills or certifications?
- What are your fees and how are they structured?
- How often will I be billed?
- Are there any additional costs that may occur? (postage, copy fees, filing fees etc.)
- Do you have a written fee agreement or representation agreement?

- Is there anyone else that would be helping on this case, and if so, what are their rates?
- Do you outsource any legal tasks?
- Do you carry malpractice insurance? If so, what is the cost?
- Are you able to provide any references from past clients?

It is important to note that a higher attorney fee does not necessarily mean the lawyer is more qualified. However, any attorney offering pricing that seems 'too good to be true' is usually a red flag. After asking your questions, consider how quickly and accurately they were able to provide you with answers. Do you feel comfortable with the fees and the structure of payments they have offered? Did you feel comfortable communicating with them? Asking the right questions will help you determine if the lawyer is a good fit for your specific case.

RETAINERS & COMMON FEES

A retainer fee is essentially a down payment on the legal services you will be receiving. It is somewhat comparable to having your attorney be 'on call.' The retainer fee is generally placed in an account and is withdrawn as the costs are incurred. There are two main types of retainers:

- An advance payment retainer is a sum you will provide to your lawyer to cover payment of legal fees expected to be incurred during the representation process. The lawyer will agree to return any fees that are not earned during the representation.
- A general retainer is a sum paid to the lawyer simply for being available to the client.

Retainer agreements between a lawyer and their client must be fair, reasonable, fully known and understood by the client. Some lawyers may request a non-refundable retainer. If you are considering paying this, ensure that you are happy with the lawyer you have chosen and are happy to work with them for the entire process. On the other hand, many attorneys will be happy for you to pay for the majority of their costs in installments.

The costs associated with your case will depend on a few things, including how cooperative you are with your attorney's fee structure and how efficient you are with communicating the information and evidence you have.

Some of the fees associated with a child custody case include:

- **Consultation fee**: some attorneys will charge a fee just to meet with you, and some do not - be sure to ask about this before scheduling your first meeting
- **A flat fee agreement**: this option may be offered if your case is fairly simple and straightforward. This fee would be specific and would not change.
- **An hourly rate**: this is the most common structure used by attorneys. It is a standard rate for an hour's worth of work, although in some cases attorneys will charge a specific rate for one type of service (such as research) and separate rate for another service (such as court appearance).
- **A referral fee**: if an attorney refers you to a different attorney, they may ask you to pay a portion of the total fee you will be paying for the case.

These fees will vary from firm to firm, as well as within different states. The fees are assessed based on the amount of work the attorney expects to put into the case and takes into consideration the difficulty of your specific situation. Typically in a child custody battle, each party is responsible for paying their own legal fees and any costs associated with their case. However, if there is a large disparity between yours and your spouse's financial status, special circumstances may be put in place, such as a Judge awarding more reasonable attorney fees.

Child custody cases are often quite complicated, so if there is ever a time to use an attorney, a custody battle is the time. An attorney's knowledge and experience will be extremely helpful in navigating such an important process in your family's life.

FINANCING YOUR CASE

The combination of filing for divorce and attempting to gain custody of your child can be very expensive. It will likely cost thousands of dollars, so the sooner you can start setting aside money, the better. If you share bank accounts with your spouse and have a feeling that a divorce is in your future, it can be helpful to slowly start withdrawing funds as early as possible to build up some extra savings.

If you do not have a lot of savings available to you, consider any and all options available. Borrow from friends and family, sell valuable items (such as jewelry), or cash in investments. The cost may be high, but it is well worth it to ensure your child will end up in the best living environment possible. Get creative doing whatever is necessary to build up your savings, and rest assured that it will be money well spent.

Some parents worry that their income may affect the outcome of their case. If you make significantly less money than your spouse, that doesn't mean you will be deemed less fit to parent your children. Instead, the court may award a higher amount of child support to ensure that you are enabled to support your child financially. The court's goal in awarding child support is always to keep the child's quality of living as close to what is was prior to the divorce.

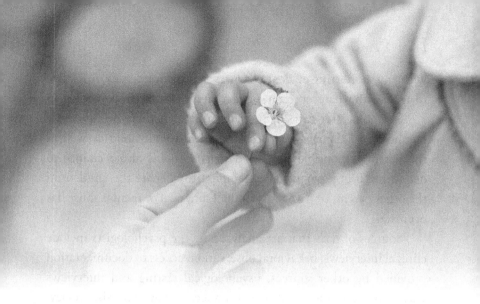

PSYCHOLOGISTS

THEIR ROLE IN THE CASE

Psychologists can help with custody battles in a number of ways. The use of psychological testing in a child custody battle can be paramount to building your case. They will often evaluate both the child (or children) and parents to determine if there are any concerning behavior patterns or negative personality traits that could be detrimental to the lives of the children involved.

The use of psychological testing in child custody evaluations can be extremely important, and many people involved place a lot of weight on these tests, including Judges. For this reason, psychologists need take a lot of consideration in terms of which tests are developmentally and culturally appropriate to use in each specific situation. Many factors within a custody case are hard to quantify and test results should be used more as a hypothesis in collaboration with any supporting evidence. However, it is common for the Judge to agree with whatever recommendation is made by the psychologist.

Psychologists can help determine whether or not any psychological damage has occurred within your child as well as the parent responsible for that damage. This is also a chance to determine if any parent has attempted to alienate the child from the other parent, or if any misconduct, physical or mental abuse has occurred.

Sources of data that are analyzed by the psychologists include clinical interviews, behavioral observation, access to documentation provided by other sources, psychological testing and interviews with family, friends and acquaintances. They will also review any prior mental health records or existing conditions. Based on everything they review, they will create a recommendation that will be given to the Judge who will decide whether or not to allow that recommendation to become the outcome of the case.

In 1994, the American Psychological Association developed the **Guidelines for Child Custody Evaluations in Divorce Proceedings.** These guidelines were created for psychologists to have a systematic framework to ensure a high level of practice. The guidelines are as follows:

- The purpose of the evaluation is to assist the psychologist in determining the best interests of the child.
- The child's welfare is paramount.
- The evaluation should focus on the parenting attributes and the child's psychological needs.
- Psychologists should strive to:
  o Gain and maintain specialized competence.
  o Function as impartial evaluators.
  o Engage in practices that are culturally informed, and nondiscriminatory
  o Avoid conflicts of interest and multiple relationships when conducting evaluations.

○ Establish the scope of the evaluation in a timely fashion and should remain consistent with the nature of the referral question.

○ Obtain the appropriately informed consent.

○ Employ a number of methods of data gathering.

○ Interpret assessment data in a manner consistent with the context of the evaluation.

○ Complement the evaluation with the appropriate combination of examinations.

○ Base their recommendations upon the best psychological interests of the child.

• Psychologists should create and maintain professional records that are in line with their ethical and legal obligations.

WHAT THEY LOOK FOR

In the most basic sense, psychologists are concerned with Maslow's Hierarchy of Needs, which, in order from most refined to most basic are:

• **Self-Actualization** - the desire to become the most that one can be
• **Esteem** - respect, self-esteem, status, recognition, strength, freedom
• **Love and Belonging** - friendship, solid family bond, sense of connection
• **Safety Needs** - personal security (emotional and physical), resources, health, property
• **Physiological Needs** - basic necessities such as air, water, food, shelter, sleep, clothing, reproduction

In summary, the psychologist wants to determine where the child will feel happiest, most comfortable and that their basic needs are going to be met. Typically, children feel more secure with a strong parent, and because of that, the psychologist will evaluate the strengths and weakness both parents possess.

Many psychologists look favorably upon parents who are more flexible and willing to compromise, rather than those that are aggressive and unwilling to negotiate from their own agenda. There are some exceptions to this. For example, if one parent is aggressive and the other is too passive, the psychologist may award custody to the aggressive parent simply due to the fact that it seems the other parent is not willing to put in any effort to fight for their child. The key is to be assertive about your strategy and goals without coming across as hostile. Psychologists do not want to see any manipulation happening between spouses and will work to determine if any inappropriate behaviors are present. This is why it is imperative to show the psychologist that you are willing to cooperate a throughout the process.

When a psychologist is court-appointed in a child custody evaluation, there are tests that will be given to the parents to determine personality traits and potential problems. These tests are usually comprised of many (up to 600) true or false statements to be answered honestly by the parents. Some of the patterns these tests analyze are tendencies toward:

- Depression
- Narcissism
- Hysteria
- Psychopathy
- Paranoia
- Hypomania
- Schizophrenia
- Manipulation
- Substance abuse
- Misconduct
- Pathological lying

- Hypochondriasis
- Criminal behavior
- Sociopathy

Ultimately, the psychologist wants to know if either parent is mentally ill or mentally stable. It is extremely important to answer any and all evaluation questions openly and honestly, as they are designed to uncover manipulation and dishonesty. If you try to answer the questions based on what you think they want to see, rather than the actual truth, your results may come across as manipulative. The psychologists are trying to determine if there are any extreme personality traits that could be hazardous in the long term to the child or children.

They will also want to know how you are coping and have coped with your divorce, and whether or not your child's well-being is at the top of your priority list. They will want to know *why* you want custody; is it out of spite or revenge? Or do you truly believe that you are the better parent to raise your child. If it is the latter, make sure that you showcase that to the psychologist as well as during the entire child custody process.

PERSONALITY DISORDERS

The definition of personality is the basic patterns, traits and behaviors that define or characterize an individual. Generally, healthy and well-adjusted adults are able to adjust to changes within their lives, whether it is mentally or physically. Some adults struggle with change and prove to be ill-equipped to cope with these changes and develop unhealthy patterns or behaviors as a result.

A personality disorder is a specific disorder in which the individual has a rigid and unhealthy pattern of thinking, functioning or behavior. This person will likely have trouble perceiving and relating to typical situations and may have issues or abnormalities when communicating with others. Someone with a personality disorder will think, feel and behave in a way that deviates from cultural expectations and norms. In many cases, this can have a negative effect on their ability to parent effectively. Certain personality disorders can overlap, such as narcissism and sociopathy. A psychologist's role is to determine if any and how many personality disorders are present within the parents involved in the case. This will help them begin to understand which parent would be better suited to have custodial rights.

Keeping track of your partner's behaviors can be helpful information to provide to the psychologist, because it may help them confirm the findings they discover within their evaluations. If you have any pre-existing diagnoses or conditions, it is important to be upfront and disclose them. It is even more important to show what steps you currently have put into place to keep any negative effects on your life and the lives of your children to a minimum.

EVALUATIONS

The psychologist will only spend a small amount of time with each of the parties in your case, so it is important to prepare as much evidence as possible prior to meeting with them. You should work diligently with your attorney to provide the psychologist any and all compelling evidence you have supporting your case. You want them to have as much information as possible *before* they do their evaluations

The results you get from any preliminary testing done by the psychologist will affect how thoroughly you will be evaluated. Doing well on the evaluation does not ensure that you will win the custody battle, but it is highly beneficial for your case. As mentioned, the psychologist's results and recommendations are weighed heavily when it comes to the final decision by the Judge.

Every evaluation will be unique, but here are some general tips to keep in mind:

- Arrive on time or early and dressed appropriately for all evaluations
- For any written tests, read all questions carefully and answer them honestly
- During evaluations, listen carefully to each question and answer them honestly
- Refer to your child or children as 'ours' rather than 'mine'
- Have your attorney provide all relevant evidence and share your journal with them prior to testing
- Don't use derogatory words when describing your spouse
- Keep any negative emotions to a minimum and show that you are willing to cooperate during the process
- Ensure you emphasize that the best interests of your child or children is your top priority

FORENSIC EVALUATIONS

A custody forensic evaluation is performed by a licensed mental health professional, and tare only needed in some cases. These evaluations can only be ordered by a Judge, and they are usually ordered when the parents cannot agree on the custody arrangements. In some cases, the Judge will ask the attorney representing the children if they believe a forensic evaluation is necessary. If there are specific concerns about the case, there may be a request to have special attention paid to those areas, such as domestic violence, mental illness or substance abuse. In fact, it is common for these evaluations to be ordered if there are allegations of those very things.

Forensic evaluators are independent neutral third-parties whose sole focus is providing unbiased information to the Judge. The evaluators are usually a psychologist, psychiatrist or social worker, and have a large portion of their background devoted to forensics. The evaluation results usually influence the Judge's decision, but while they do carry a heavy weight, they do not directly ensure the same results within the custody. The results the evaluators provide are intended to be an impartial analysis and suggestion in what arrangements they feel would suit the children's best interests.

If a forensic evaluation has been ordered in your case, it is always in your best interests to comply. If you choose not to participate, it will look extremely unfavorable in the eyes of the Judge. As with all aspects of your child custody battle, be respectful of any evaluators and cooperative throughout the process. Any negative or hostile behaviors will only act as a detriment to your case. Be open, calm and honest and remember why you are in this battle; to fight for the rights of your child or children.

Everyone involved in the case will participate in an initial meeting where they will meet with the evaluator alone. These meetings are used to gather background information on the case, and will sometimes include psychological testing. Following the initial interview will be a joint child-parent meeting. The purpose of these interviews is for the evaluator to observe the interactions between parents and their children. Both you and your spouse will have separate joint child-parent meeting. Depending on the age of your children, there may also be meetings where the children will be interviewed by the evaluator alone. Any stepparents or new partners will also be asked to participate in certain parts of the evaluations. Once completed, the forensic report will be admitted as evidence to be used within the custody hearing.

Some other important information surrounding forensic evaluations are:

- They can be a lengthy process, sometimes taking as long as 4 months from start to finish. There is a significant amount of information gathered within these evaluations, and it is in your child's best interests that it is done thoroughly and correctly.

- There is a fee involved in the evaluation process, and both parents should expect to be billed a pro-rated fee based on each of their incomes.

- If there is an order of protection involved in your case, the interviews will be adjusted. Children will not have to be interviewed with any parent who has an order placed against them.

- Do not coach your children on what to say within the interviews. It is, however, important to prepare them for the interviews. Explain to them that they will be talking with a doctor, and that it is important to answer all questions as honestly as they can. It may help to tell them that you and your spouse will be talking to the doctor as well, so they know they are not going through this process alone.

- Interviews must be conducted in person, not virtually or over the phone.

- Remember that these evaluations are not about your marriage and the problems you are facing there; it is an evaluation about the parenting abilities of you and your spouse.

It is in your best interests to come to any and all meetings and evaluations prepared. Make sure you are clear on what information the evaluator has requested in order to complete their reports, and bring it with you to the interviews. Some of the things you may be asked to provide include:

- **Documentation**: this can include report cards, medical records, relevant emails, etc.
- **Collateral Evidence**: this evidence can consist of interviews with people outside of your immediate family but who are active within the lives of your children. These people could

be teachers, doctors, neighbors, babysitters, coaches, etc. If this evidence is requested, you will likely be asked to provide a list of all names and contact information so the evaluator can conduct interviews with those people.

- **Paperwork**: If you have been asked by the evaluator to complete any paperwork or fill out any questionnaires, be sure to bring completed copies of that paperwork.

- **Journal**: You may find it helpful to bring any notes you have taken prior to the evaluations to ensure you don't forget any important information, including any questions you may have for the evaluator.

BUILDING YOUR CASE

PREPARING YOUR CASE

You can never be too prepared when it comes to battling for custody of your child. Any and all evidence you can gather on your own, even before contacting an investigator or lawyer, will be helpful to the preparation of your case. The key is to ensure that all evidence you gather is honest and accurate. Preparing for your case is a prime example of how keeping a consistent journal can go a long way. Regardless of how many experts you add to your support system, **you** are the expert of your case. You will have the best understanding of which witnesses will be most beneficial to interview, what elements should take priorities over others and specific routes to investigate more thoroughly. Not all child custody cases actually end up going to trial, and if you have enough solid evidence prepared, you may save yourself a lot of time and money. Preparing for your case includes the following steps:

- Creating and maintaining a consistent journal
- Performing an investigation (and potentially hiring an investigator)
- Finding a qualified attorney
- Filing for custody
- Appointing a psychologist
- Preparing for psychological evaluations
- Interviewing witnesses
- Preparing those witnesses
- Collecting and disclosing all relevant evidence
- Preparing for trial

There are 5 main elements within a child custody case: parents, children, lawyers, psychologists and the Judge. A term you will learn to become familiar with is **discovery**. The discovery within a case is comprised of any facts, documents or other information that can and will be used during the trial. Discovery can include many things, such as criminal records, driving records, police reports, school records, health records, witness interviews and depositions. Organizing and prioritizing this information is very important and is something that you can help your attorney in doing. This includes staying on top of all new information that presents itself once the process has started, and effectively communicating that information with the parties who require it. When you are communicating with your lawyer, investigator and psychologist, the strategy should always be to uncover the truth. This is especially important if you believe your spouse is unfit to parent. If that is the case, ideally the truth you are trying to expose is that you are the best parent to raise your child. This will take a combination of legal maneuvering, meticulous investigation and solid documentation to expose any weaknesses or negative parenting traits in your spouse.

Aside from keeping a journal of events, your case will begin with an investigation. You likely wouldn't file for custody if everything was amicable between you and your spouse, and you had no concerns about their ability to effectively parent your child. You can hire an investigator to do the discreet research that will prove essential in building your case. They will research everything from school records and police records to general inappropriate habits and behaviors. Certain information will only be available to parents due to varying privacy laws, so information that falls under that category will be your responsibility to provide. The investigator will help with the rest.

An investigation can be very helpful, especially because it can be done before your partner is aware that you are attempting to file for custody of your child. This element of surprise can be very effective, because any information gathered against your spouse will be candid and authentic; it will not be tainted by them trying to act in a certain way knowing that they are being investigated. Once you have found an attorney to add to your team, you can provide them with any evidence you have collected, along with the evidence collected by the investigator. This will be a great foundation for them to start building your case.

Once the child custody process has begun, the Judge will appoint a psychologist to evaluate the parents and children involved. An investigative report can be helpful to provide to the psychologist, and this is something you can request your attorney do on your behalf. Because the psychologist's recommendation carries such a significant influence on the final decision of the Judge, it is essential to prepare thoroughly for the psychological evaluation. Your attorney can help ensure you are ready for this process.

Take your time with the preparation, especially during the investigation. Any relevant information uncovered through the investigation will be disclosed to the Judge as well as to your spouse and their legal team. Without a comprehensive investigation, your chances of winning the case diminishes greatly. Within the trial itself, there will be no jury; the outcome of the case will be based on your evidence, any psychological evaluations and finally, the decision of the Judge.

KEEPING AN EFFECTIVE JOURNAL

Keeping a consistent and accurate journal has been mentioned in this guide multiple times, and for good reason. A journal will be one of the first and most crucial assets when building your case. Your journal represents a chronology of events that can help to explain your partner's ineffective patterns and behaviors, that may not be evident to others (or even to you at first). For example, your spouse may present themselves as very cool, calm and collected to most people, but are quick to be angry or violent without provocation. This could be evidence of borderline personality disorder. Maybe your spouse is completely consumed with themselves and their own well-being and show a lack of empathy or guilt. This could be evidence of sociopathy or narcissism. Any information you gather can be extremely helpful to the psychologist assigned to your case, especially if it supports the evidence that they find through their own evaluation. Proving mental illness does not ensure you will win, but having consistent documented evidence of negative behaviors will definitely add to supporting your case.

It is important that you apply the mindset of using logic over emotion when writing in your journal, as you do not want it to seem like you are setting up a trap or providing biased information. Try and keep it strictly informative, leaving emotion out of it whenever you can. A psychologist will likely be able to discern if you have crafted a 'story' about your spouse rather than a collection of accurate and detailed events. Because of this, you can also include some positive aspects of your spouse's parenting skills, or maybe elude to the fact that they used to behave more appropriately but you have noticed a decline in those skills over the years.

While it is important to note events as they occur in real time, it can be helpful to include information about the beginning of your relationship, especially if you notice there have been significant changes in your spouse as the years have gone by. Details like this can be very helpful, especially to the psychologist, so they can understand a synopsis of sorts between you and your spouse. Be sure to include any and all information that could be relevant to your case, especially any physical or mental abuse, alcohol or substance abuse, violent episodes, etc. This will help prepare the psychologist in terms of the questions they will ask your spouse when evaluating them, and they may be able to expose more truths with that background information.

Here are some general tips for keeping an effective journal:

- Include a table of contents if possible, to make navigating through the information easy
- Double space the content and write as clearly as possible
- Write chronologically when possible, and highlight important facts and details
- Include all relevant times, dates and locations (and, if possible, back up the information with receipts, reports, tickets, etc.)
- Identify and explain the roles of any important people involved in your writing
- This can also be a great place to store any police or investigative reports

TABLE OF CONTENTS

It may seem unnecessary or excessive to include a table of contents within your journal, but it can be very helpful, especially when a third party is reviewing your information. You can include headings such as 'outbursts, substance abuse, infidelity, manipulation, alienation' etc. It is important to note that a journal doesn't have to be written in a leather-bound book; if it is easier for you to organize information, you can create a file folder of information to separate the information into sections. The term journal will be used in this guide to refer to anywhere you are able to collect accurate and consistent evidence.

CHRONOLOGY AND HIGHLIGHTING KEY DETAILS

The events you document in your journal should be organized in chronological order when possible. However, this doesn't mean you have to actually write every page in chronological order. If you remember an incident that occurred in the past, you can still write about it now, just be sure to catalog it in a way that accurately represents the time in which the events occurred. It is important to always include time and date stamps with everything you write, to help create a true timeline of events. It is also important to be transparent about the dates and times you are writing about - meaning if you are writing about an event that happened in the past, you can include the day in which it happened but also include the date in which you are writing about it.

Just as it is important to ensure that your notes are detailed and accurate, they need to be legible and easy for someone else to navigate through. If your attorney or psychologist consistently find that they cannot read what you have written, they may overlook and discount certain pages or even sections. You are keeping track of this information for a reason, and it needs to be clear and neatly kept. Be sure to accentuate key facts and details, either by highlighting or keeping color coded tabs on those specific sections.

IDENTIFY IMPORTANT WITNESSES

The journal is going to act as the story between you and your spouse and, as such, it is important to include any relevant 'characters' and the roles they play. This can be especially helpful when determining the people you want to act as witnesses on your behalf, and those who may be detrimental to your case. You are going to need to build a list of friends, family and acquaintances who are familiar with the events that have taken place between you and your spouse. Feel free to identify the strengths and weaknesses of any relevant people as well as any relationship they have or have had with your children. Keep in mind that unbiased witnesses are usually the most compelling when taking the stand during your trial.

Keeping a journal is especially effective when your spouse doesn't portray any obvious negative patterns or behaviors, or when they are very good at hiding those traits. These organized notes make it much easier to identify the flaws that may not be evident to someone who is on the outside looking in. This journal can help you and all of the people on your support team, and it will act as the foundation for every aspect in your case.

INVESTIGATION

The evidence gathered by investigation can make or break a case. You have the potential to uncover many factors that the court will take into consideration when determining the best interests of your child. There are three main techniques that are used by investigators to gather evidence:

- **Surveillance**
- Photographs, video, monitoring or 'tailing' a parent's incidences of neglect, abuse or other mistreatment

- **Background Searches**
- Criminal records, lawsuits, financial problems, and substance abuse

- **Witness Statements**
- Information to establish character, suitability, conduct and an overall ability to parent

Surveillance is one of the most expensive and difficult parts involved in an investigation, and it is important to employ a qualified and experienced investigator. As long as the evidence is obtained in a legal matter, it can be presented to the court. Your investigator should be well versed in the legality behind gathering this information. Evidence can be gathered in many ways such as written reports, audio recordings, and videotapes. Generally speaking, if you collect proof of behaviors that threaten the best interests and welfare of your child, it will be accepted as evidence within your case.

Many people mistakenly assume that attorneys are also investigators. While an attorney may be able to gather some information on their own, depending on the complexity of your situation, hiring a qualified investigator can be beneficial. Some attorneys will be able to recommend an investigator for your case. When possible, get a referral from someone, whether it is a friend, family member, or even another attorney (if your attorney doesn't have direct contact with one). Always ask any potential investigator about their experience working on child custody cases. Keep in mind though, that they don't necessarily need to have experience with child custody cases to be helpful in your situation. There are a few qualities that are shared by the best investigators:

- They have a good appearance, but don't stand out. This is especially important if they going to be tailing your spouse
- They are good listeners
- They pay close attention to detail and are analytical
- They are easy to talk to, and do not have an abrupt personality. This is especially important when considering the specific people you will you want them to interview

There are also some red flags to look out for. Here are 5 things your investigator should not request, report, or demand are:

1. That you and your spouse should never say anything negative about the other parent, and if you do then you will lose custody. This demand, or requirement, is unfair and diminishes the importance of your emotions.

2. That your ex's behavior is allowed, but that yours is not. If you and your ex are doing or saying similar things but the investigator is clearly favoring one over another, that is grounds for further examination on your part. If the investigator has a clear favorite and their mis-behavior is going unchecked, you have a right to say something.

3. That things "out of bounds" will be evaluated, such as assessing your home, or your psychology, when that is not their field or when they weigh something with heavy importance that is not part of the evaluation.

4. That they need to spend more or less time with one parent over another. An inequality of time spent in evaluations an change the outcome of their judgement. If the "favorite" parent is not given a thorough evaluation, there is a possibility that the evaluation is inaccurate and detrimental to the stability of your children's care. In contrast, if the favorite is given substantially more time, then that parent can sway the investigator's opinion and result in his or her favor.

5. That one parent is all good or all bad. Absolutes do not exist in the world of parenting and should not appear in custody evaluations. One parent may bring out the worst in another, but that does not mean that the "bad" parent is bad 100% of the time. Your assets and your weaknesses should be included in your report, as should your ex.

There are a few other ways to gather evidence through investigation, such doing a 'trash audit' by searching your spouse's trash. You will want to ensure that there are no state laws restricting you (and your investigator) from doing this. In most states, the constitution's 4th Amendment does not prohibit the search and seizure of garbage which has been left for collection outside of a home, even without a warrant. This can be a very effective way of gathering a multitude of evidence. If you do choose to investigate in this manner, be sure to so in an inconspicuous way, as to not incite any further issues from your spouse or to tip them off, which could prevent further evidence from being collected.

If you use an investigator in your case, they can be a crucial member of your team, and paramount in building a case against your spouse. Be sure to keep open lines of communications with all parties involved to make sure all evidence collection is being done efficiently and effectively.

PREPARING WITNESSES

Witnesses may prove to be one of the most important aspects of your case. Because of the weight their testimonies will hold, you need to ensure all of your witnesses are fully prepared for trial. The information provided by the witnesses in their testimonies can make or break a case. There have been cases in the past where a parent chooses a witness to testify on their behalf, and that witness ends up destroying their case, because they simply were not aware or prepared enough to present the information accurately. On top of that, testifying in a courtroom in from of a Judge can be extremely nerve-racking, even for someone who is knowledgeable on what they are speaking about.

Witnesses are always sworn in before testifying, and it is important that they honor that oath. Testifying on behalf of someone doesn't mean saying whatever you think the Judge wants to hear. There are certain tactics your spouse's lawyer may use when interviewing your witness to try and twist their words. They also may ask questions to undermine the credibility of your witness, or pressure them into saying something that they will be able to use in their own favor.

When helping to prepare your witnesses for trial, it is important to provide as much background information about your case as possible, so they do not get caught off guard during questioning. Remind them to listen carefully to the questions being asked of them, and to answer all questions as directly as possible. The more time you spend preparing each witness before the trial, the better.

Make sure they know exactly what your strategy is, and share any documentation you feel may be helpful for them to better understand your specific situation. Your attorney can help to let you know the kinds of questions that will be asked, the difference between a direct examination and a cross-examination, and the difference between open-ended and leading questions.

Before you choose the witnesses to testify on your behalf, it is important to evaluate how effective they will really be. When evaluating your potential witnesses, it can be helpful to organize and prioritize them based on their importance to your case, as well as what information they are able to testify about. There will very likely be personal questions asked of the witnesses, such as whether or not they would leave their own children with one of the parents in the case. They need to be able to answer these questions calmly and effectively, so their answers do not come across as biased or rehearsed.

MISTAKES TO AVOID

One of the first (and most common) errors people make when preparing for a child custody battle is failing to use the element of surprise. You are able to gather the most unbiased and candid information when your spouse doesn't know you are doing so. As soon as they are aware that they are being investigated, there is a chance that they will change their behaviors or 'put on a show.'

Another common mistake is not taking the time to educate yourself about the process. Most people don't go through multiple custody battles, so it is completely normal if you don't know a lot about how the process works. Take the time to research the do's and don'ts, reach out to others who have already gone through the process, and make a list of questions to ask your attorney, investigator and psychologist before choosing to work with them. Make sure every member of your support system is as prepared as possible to ensure you have the best chance for getting the outcome you desire.

It is also very important to avoid venting any frustrations on social media during the child custody battle. Once an image, video or post is uploaded onto a social media platform, they can be accessed by anyone and then copied or reproduced to be used as evidence against you. Even if you think what you are posting is unrelated to your case, be extremely cautious about anything and everything you upload before your trial is complete. You can never know what your spouse's attorney will use to try and spin the case against you.

Depending on your situation, the court may issue temporary court orders until the dispute is able to go to trial. These interim orders can determine the temporary parental rights of both parties, among other things. While these orders may be temporary, they are legally enforceable. If a parent chooses to disobey any of these orders, it could lead to a court violation, which can impact the Judge's final decision for the outcome of your case.

Finally, it is essential to showcase that you are cooperative and willing to communicate openly. A child custody battle can feel very personal, and it is easy to let the emotions you are feeling cloud your judgement and focus. Many parents make the mistake of trying to fully alienate their spouse during the process. Refraining from that kind of behavior is especially important if there are any temporary orders that include time-sharing with your partner. You are more than likely going to encounter situations where both you and your spouse must be present and communicative with each other.

If you refuse communication, you may come across as stubborn or combative, which can be frowned upon by the psychologist as well as the Judge. Even if you are not happy with the custody arrangements, any negative emotions you are feeling should be left to discuss between you and your attorney. Whenever possible, and especially when in the presence of your spouse and their attorney, be on your absolute best behavior. Winning your case will come down to the evidence you gather against your spouse, and the way in which your parenting ability is perceived by the psychologist and Judge.

PROVING YOUR CASE

INTERVIEWING

There are two main types of interviews that can be used: face-to-face and over the phone. Both options can be effective and certain people will prefer one over the other. Your investigator will also be able to suggest which type is best for different personality types. The background information you provide about each witness will help them know how to approach the interview. Whichever route is chosen, you must ensure that all interviews are documented. Be sure you (and your investigator) are familiar with state recording laws, because recording without consent is illegal in some places. If that is the case where you are located, you can have each witness sign a statement providing their consent.

Some states have 'no-fault' divorces; in those cases, the lifestyles of the parents involved would be irrelevant. When children are involved, the lifestyle of each parent is always relevant and very important. It is essential to have witnesses that can attest to the positive aspects of your lifestyle and parenting skills, as well as those who can attest to any negative parenting skills, behaviors and lifestyle choices your spouse has. If you know of a specific negative quality or habit your spouse has, it is extremely important to have as many people as possible corroborate that information.

Try to organize any potential interviews in terms of priority and chronologically. For example, it makes more sense to interview former babysitters before interviewing present ones. When possible, it is also beneficial to interview witnesses before your spouse and their attorney have a chance to connect with them first, and potentially influence their story. It is crucial to document every interview in case people change their story when it comes time to testify. Interviews can be the perfect way to catch people in a lie, which goes a long way in terms of ruining someone's credibility within your case.

If you have reason to believe your spouse may have been unfaithful in your relationship, witnesses may be able to help or prove that as well. In a no-fault divorce state, adultery is not a big issue, but during a child custody battle, it can be a major issue. Using your journal as a reference, and with your attorney's guidance, you should be able to prioritize exactly what topics should be discussed with each witness. These interviews can help uncover or confirm information that will prove monumental in determining the outcome of your case. As with the rest of the custody process, make sure you have provided as much information as possible to all parties involved in order to maximize the effectiveness of the interviewing process.

NEGLECT

Neglect is defined by a pattern of failing to provide for a child's basic needs. In a way, it is abuse through the omission of meeting those needs. Proving neglect can be complex as it is much harder to identify than something like physical abuse. Neglect can result in serious mental and physical health issues, and in extreme cases, death.

While it can be a bit ambiguous, there are several ways that neglect can be noticed and confirmed, including if the child:

- Appears to be consistently dirty and unkempt
- Lacks appropriate medical attention, whether it is dental or medical (not having immunizations, glasses etc.)
- Is frequently absent from school and/or extra-curricular activities
- Lacks appropriate clothing for weather conditions
- Consistently mentions that they are hungry or not being taken care of

In extreme cases, it will be necessary to get Child Protective Services involved quickly, and if you are in the midst of your custody battle, it can be done on behalf of the court. The agency can then testify on behalf of the child during the trial. If this pertains to your case, your attorney will be able to help you work with the agency to involve them in an appropriate manner. If your spouse has been neglecting your child, it will greatly impact your likelihood of winning custody. More importantly, it will allow that child to escape those unhealthy conditions and return to an environment that is safe and comfortable for them to live. This should always be the primary objective in any child custody case.

There are only so many hours in a day; for 6-8 hours during the day, most parents are working, and most children are in school. For another 8 hours they are all likely asleep, leaving only a few hours a day for parents to actually spend time with their kids. What a parent chooses to do with those hours during the week and during the weekends speaks volumes to their parenting priorities and abilities.

Unfortunately, many times when you investigate parental neglect, it can turn into proving abuse. The two often go hand in hand, especially when a parent has issues with substance abuse; the addiction becomes the priority and the child's needs slip through the cracks. Being aware of what your spouse is choosing to do with their time when they could be spending it with your child can help to build a case for neglect. The combination of the information gathered by your investigator and the work done by the psychologist, will help to support this possibility. Physical neglect leads to mental neglect and, when this is done constantly and consistently, it can turn into abuse. It is important for a child to grow up in an environment that allows them to flourish in all aspects, while feeling safe and comfortable. The safety and well-being of the child is vital to their mental and physical health. Any environment where this is not the primary focus, is not conducive to raising a healthy and happy child.

CHILD ABUSE

Abuse can occur in many forms and unfortunately, there are often times two or more types may go hand in hand. There are four main categories when it comes to child abuse:

- Neglect
- Physical Abuse
- Emotional/Mental Abuse
- Sexual Abuse

Physical abuse is the non-accidental infliction of physical injury to a child. It is often characterized by injuries the child incurs, including bruising, lesions, fractures, and burns among other things. While the actions need to be non-accidental, even if the parent does not consciously intend to cause injury, it is still considered abuse. One example of a specific type of child abuse is Shaken Baby Syndrome (SBS). This is caused by violent shaking of a baby, often done in an effort to stop them from crying. It can lead to serious injuries, including tearing of the brain lining, brain bleeds, permanent brain injury or even death.

There are also other types of physical abuse that are far less obvious. Munchausen by Proxy Syndrome is when a parent wrongly convinces the child (and others) that the child is sick. This results in a seriously dysfunctional relationship between the parent and child, and some research shows it is an extreme manifestation of an attachment disorder. The parent is so desperate to keep that child close to them that they manufacture reasons to ensure the child will remain dependent on them.

Another form of physical abuse is alcohol, cigarette or other drug use during pregnancy. These actions can cause serious long-term damage to the child including Fetal Alcohol Syndrome or pre-conditioning a child to cancer, among other issues. In some cases, the child may be upfront in reporting an injury by a parent. If your child mentions this, you should always take it seriously and reach out for professional help immediately. Be sure to document all steps of this process, including the date in which it is first mentioned as well as all associated medical investigations and records.

Other indicators of physical abuse include when:

- The child has unexplained injuries that do not look like they were caused by simply playing (such as welts that are in the shape of a specific shape of an object, or cigarette burns)
- The child flinches or cowers at the approach of adults
- The child seems nervous or frightened of the parent and may not want to return to their home

Examples of possible indications that a parent is trying to cover up abuse include:

- Offering insufficient or conflicting explanations with regards to specific injuries
- Often describing the child in a negative manner
- Using harsh or unwarranted discipline with the child

There is also emotional abuse, which is defined as any attitude, behavior or failure to act that interferes with a child's social development and mental health. This is done when a parent has a repeated pattern of behavior conveying to the child that they are flawed, inadequate, unloved or unworthy. This kind of abuse includes verbal abuse and/or constant criticism, and is almost always present alongside another form of abuse. Parents who mentally abuse their children do so using more subtle tactics such as intimidation, manipulation or refusing to ever be content or appreciative toward their child. Emotional abuse can have longer lasting negative psychiatric effects than other forms of abuse.

Some of the other ways in which emotional abuse can be illustrated are:

- Terrorizing, threatening violence or fearful conditions
- Constant belittling, rejecting or bullying
- Exploiting or corrupting
- Isolating, confining or restricting the child from social interactions
- Denying the child emotional response or acknowledgment
- Deliberately ignoring the child

Emotional abuse can be identified in a variety of ways, including if the child:

- Is delayed in certain physical or emotional development
- Seems to be detached from the parent
- Show extremes in behavior - either being overly compliant or demanding, severely aggressive or extremely passive
- Acts inappropriately like an adult (trying to parent other children, another sibling or even their parent/caregiver
- Alternatively, they act inappropriately infantile, showing signs of regression such as speaking like a baby, or wanting a bottle or toy they have grown out of

While all acts of child abuse are heinous and deplorable, one of the most universally upsetting forms is sexual abuse. Sexual child abuse is defined by any sexual behavior or sexual exploitation of a child. The three main types of sexual offenses committed against children are rape, molestation and the production, distribution or possession of child pornography.

A child cannot legally give consent to sexual activity of any kind. It is an unfortunate statistic that approximately 90% of sexual abuse among children is done by a family member or someone they know. If you have reason to believe your spouse is sexually abusing your child, it is imperative to report it and do absolutely everything in your power to remove the child from the situation immediately. Involve every member of your team that can help, starting with the psychologist and any medical professionals as well as Child Protective Services if necessary. If this information is uncovered during your child custody battle, there are temporary motions the Judge can put into place to ensure the child is removed from that environment until the trial is complete.

Every parent wants to hope that their child would tell them if something inappropriate has occurred, but due to fear or intimidation by their perpetrator, that is not always the case. Some of the warning signs of sexual abuse include if a child:

- Is avoiding things related to sexuality, showing rejection or discomfort of their own body or genitals
- Displays overly sophisticated, unusual and inappropriate sexual or seductive behavior
- Has inappropriate knowledge or interest in sexual activities
- Has changes in their behavior, such as issues with discipline, bed wetting, insomnia, nightmares, changes in appetite, anxiety or depression
- Is being overly compliant or acting out with excessive aggression
- Fears a specific adult or family member

- Suddenly refuses to participate in activities that require them to change clothes
- Avoids bathrooms and/or bathing
- Isolates, shuts down or may even attempt to run away

If you notice any of these signs in your child, it is imperative that you take the child to a pediatrician to ensure no long-term physical damage is being done. It can also be helpful to take your child to a psychologist as soon as possible. The psychologist will be able to help determine what kind of psychological, physical and emotional damage has been done, and they can be a great source of support for your child while navigating through the process.

SUBSTANCE ABUSE

Issues with substance abuse are commonly seen within child custody battles and are often one of the many factors prompting a divorce. Alcoholism and drug abuse can significantly impact on someone's ability to parent in a variety of ways. Most psychologists and medical professionals agree that substance abuse is the symptom of another problem and can often go hand-in-hand with certain personality disorders. Whatever the reason may be, it can take an incredible toll on their mental and physical health as well as their family's.

ALCOHOLISM

One of the most commonly (and more socially acceptable) abused substances is alcohol. Alcoholism presents in many ways, and some people are able to hide it quite well. In some cases, it may exhibited through their lifestyle choices, such as if the individual is constantly attending social gatherings or activities where alcohol is readily available. Others may conceal their alcohol abuse better, literally hiding it in other beverages, such as in their coffee or water bottle. If you are worried that your spouse has an issue with alcohol, it is important for your child as well as your case to confirm this suspicion. Your investigator can help you do this by documenting the places and events your spouse attends and inspecting their trash and recycling. It is important to document any instances in which your spouse has been abusing alcohol when your child is under their care, especially if they have a track record for drinking and driving. Symptoms of alcoholism vary person to person, but there are a few common warning signs you can look out for, including:

- Making excuses for their drinking, such as needing to relax or deal with stress
- Experiencing short term blackouts or memory loss
- Choosing drinking over their other responsibilities and obligations
- Drinking alone or in secrecy
- Having redness in their face, or looking constantly blushed
- Weight gain, or looking like their face is swollen
- Irritability or extreme mood swings

Proving someone is abusing alcohol can be difficult, as it does not last within the body system for long, unlike some other substances. Consistent documentation of incidences as well as photo and video evidence can help you in proving your spouse has an issue with this substance.

STIMULANTS

There are several stimulant drugs that are widely used and abused. One of the most common is methamphetamine, which is often combined with pseudoephedrine (and referred to as crystal meth). It is a highly addictive and potent stimulant that wreaks havoc on the central nervous system. It has similar effects to cocaine but is significantly cheaper. Many people actually make it in their own homes. Due to its accessibility and price, methamphetamine is a drug that is used across all socioeconomic classes. There are also several prescription stimulants that are widely abused.

Common signs of stimulant use and abuse include:

- Dilated pupils
- Restlessness
- Hyperactivity
- Loss of appetite
- Weight loss
- Sweating
- Deceptive behavior, such as lying or stealing
- Using prescriptions more than prescribed
- Doctor shopping, or meeting with multiple doctors to get prescriptions
- Exhibiting excessive energy or motivation
- Aggressive behavior or anger outbursts
- Mood-swings
- Risky or impulsive behaviors
- Rapid heartbeat
- Flight of ideas and/or racing thoughts
- Anxiety or nervousness
- Increased sense of well-being or confidence

Long-term effects of stimulant abuse include increased risk of cardiac arrest, stroke, and cardiac arrhythmia. More pertinently, they can significantly one's ability to be a positive and effective parent. As with alcoholism, it can be difficult to prove that your spouse has issues with stimulant abuse. One of the most common drug tests used is a urinalysis or a urine drug test. Unfortunately, these tests can only detect the use of most drugs within three to five days of use. Very few drugs remain detectable in the system past a few days, with the exception of marijuana, which can stay in the system for up to thirty days.

If you have reason to believe your spouse is abusing any substance and wish to have them drug tested during the custody process, consider requesting a hair follicle drug test. This is the most accurate way to detect chronic substance abuse and can detect certain substances up to several months after use. It will be more difficult to find a competent lab that will administer this type of test, but the effort will be well worth it if you are struggling to prove this issue. Using the evidence you provide within your journal as well as any witnesses who are able to corroborate this information will be beneficial as well. If you are successful in proving that your spouse has a substance abuse problem or addiction, it will be a monumental step forward in your case.

THE TRIAL

If you have spent adequate time preparing for your case, collecting evidence with your investigator and attorney, and working diligently with your witnesses, the trial is when all of the pieces come together. You will present the information you have gathered to the Judge, who will then determine whether or not the case will need to go to trial. Your team may have gathered sufficient evidence to be granted custody without going to court.

If you do go to trial, that will be your opportunity to present your case fully, and the Judge will make their decision based on the 'balance of probabilities.' This simply means your evidence has to be more solid and believable than your partner's.

Your attorney will be able to help you prepare for trial, but here are some general examples of good practice when in a courtroom:

- Arrive early or at least on time, dressed appropriately
- Always stand up when speaking to the Judge and remove your hat if you are wearing one

- Don't chew gum (or anything else)
- Make sure your cell phone is on silent or off
- Be respectful and polite at all times
- Listen thoroughly to all questions and respond as clearly and directly as possible
- Refrain from any negative body language or remarks directed at your spouse or their witnesses when they are speaking

The trial will begin with opening statements, where you or your attorney will summarize the issues in your situation, explain what you are asking for and a general idea of the evidence you will presenting to support your case. You will not present any specific evidence in your opening statement; it will simply be a general summary. If you initiated this custody process, you will go first and your spouse will respond. As the trial proceeds, both you and your spouse will introduce your evidence, which will be examined via questions and answers. Questions about the evidence that are directed to witnesses will generally be open-ended questions so they are not leading in any way.

CROSS-EXAMINATION

You and your spouse will have the opportunity to cross-examine the witnesses. This means you will be able to ask your own questions to the witnesses your spouse has brought, and vice versa. The purpose of a cross examination is to bring into question the validity and credibility of their witnesses. If you have presented evidence in your case, your partner or their attorney will be allowed to cross-examine you as well. You will also have a chance to **re-examine** any witnesses to clear anything up that was mentioned during a cross-examination.

Once all evidence has been presented, and all witnesses have been examined, you and your partner will give your closing statement. In this statement, you should give another summary of your evidence, emphasize anything important that the witnesses have said, and reiterate why you believe you are the more suitable parent to raise your children.

The Judge may make their decision right at the end of the trial, or they may make their decision later, which is called 'reserving judgment.' There are a few reasons they may choose the latter, and those reasons would be based on the complexity of your case, the evidence that was presented as well as the number of other cases the Judge is currently hearing.

After the Judge has issued his or her decision, it is not enforceable until it is written and signed as an official order. If you are not happy with the decision that is reached after your trial, you can file an 'appeal'. An appeal is a request to have a higher court change or reverse the judgment in your trial.

During an appeal, the entire case will be reviewed by a higher court, and they will look at all the evidence that was presented to see if any legal errors were made. It will not be a 'do-over' of your trial, and you will not be able to submit any new evidence. They will only examine the evidence that was provided to the Judge in your original trial. It is important to note that appeals can be complicated, expensive and time-consuming. It is highly recommended you speak at length with your lawyer to discuss whether or not it is something you should proceed with.

ADDITIONAL INFORMATION

PATERNAL RIGHTS

It is commonly thought that fathers have a disadvantage in custody disputes. While statistically fathers tend to receive less custody time, simply being male does not mean you do not have a chance at winning custody of your child. If you are a father reading this guide looking to obtain custody of your child, it is even more important for you to do the necessary steps when preparing for your case.

Here are some important tips to help give you the best chance of winning your case:

1. BE ACTIVE

Leading up to and during your case, it is important for you to play an active and positive role in your child's life. Attend all important school and social gatherings and make an effort to reach out and make a good impression with other adults in your child's life such as teachers, coaches and tutors. The more people who see you being a positive and active parent in your child's life the more people you will have available to testify on your behalf.

2. PROVIDE A SAFE SPACE

No matter your living conditions, it is important to create a special place in your home devoted to your child and their belongings. A court may inquire about whether or not the parents have adequate living accommodations during the hearing, and you should be prepared to show that you do have a special place in your home suitable for your child.

3. HAVE A SOLID PLAN AND ACCURATE RECORDS

It is crucial for you to keep consistent and accurate records of all events that transpire prior to and during your case. You need to show that you have a consistent track record of being a positive influence and are present within your child's life. Keep your notes organized and showcase exactly what you have done and continue to do. Create a parenting plan to outline what you plan on doing to ensure your child's best interests in the future.

4. BE RESPECTFUL

Even if your relationship with your spouse is tumultuous, it is very important to remain respectful toward them throughout the custody process. The custody battle is not the time to vent any frustrations you have toward them, it is a time to show that you are able to remain calm and cooperative, and do whatever needs to be done to ensure your child's well-being is at the top of your priority list.

Consider reaching out to other men who are going through or have already gone through the custody process. More than ever, try to form and maintain a strong bond with your child. If you are the best person to raise your child, and you are able to present your case effectively in support of that, the Judge should grant you custody.

GRANDPARENTS

There are several reasons that grandparents may want to file for custody of their grandchildren, and in some cases, parents may even consent to the grandparents receiving custody. In other cases, both parents may be unfit to be suitable caretakers in their children's lives. In all child custody cases, the courts are attempting to determine what custody arrangement will be best for the children involved. If both parents struggle with substance abuse issues, then the grandparents will have a better chance at gaining custody. If this is the case, be sure you begin the process of gathering evidence before you start the custody process, as many parents will try to either clean up their act or at least cover up any incriminating details of their lives.

There are a few things to keep in mind when deciding if you want to gain custody of your grandchildren. If the child is placed in foster care or put up for adoption, there is a high probability that the grandparents will lose their visitation rights altogether. Be sure to research the laws in your state to see what applies to your situation. There is also something called 'guardianship' which means the parents will sign the children over temporarily to the grandparents until they are able to provide better living conditions in their home. If that is the case, the grandparents will have both physical and legal custody during that period. When time period is over, there will be a hearing to determine if the parents have done enough to regain custody of the children.

This process will be lengthy and costly with no guarantee of winning, so it is important to think carefully before beginning the process. Consider if becoming effective 'parents' to your grandchildren is something you can financially, physically and emotionally handle.

IMPEACHING THE PSYCHOLOGIST

If the court-appointed psychologist in your case renders a decision that you feel is unfair or incorrect, it is important to know that you do have another option. The psychologist's recommendation carries a large weight on the decision of the Judge, so if you feel they have been negligent or missed some key information, it is important to do everything you can to make that right. This is a perfect example of why it is so critical to have a <u>qualified attorney on your team</u>.

The first thing to investigate is the evaluations that were completed by the psychologist. The attorney can request to subpoena the notes and, in some cases, it may be beneficial to hire a second psychologist to review them. It will be important to evaluate the credibility of the witnesses who were evaluated, as well as if there were enough evaluations done to gather sufficient and accurate evidence. A second psychologist or even a pediatrician will be able to assess whether the notes taken by the psychologist and their recommendations are consistent and appropriate.

You also have the option of filing a complaint with the court or the psychology board, to help ensure the psychologist faces the consequences they deserve based on their actions. Your attorney will help to ensure that there is no bias intertwined in the psychologist's report and that they have the necessary qualifications to have been participating in the trial in the first place. Your attorney will also help to act as a neutral party to let you know if there truly has been wrongdoing, or if the psychologist simply pointed out accurate information that you may not have wanted to hear.

CHILD SUPPORT

In the majority of cases, one parent will be granted primary custody of the child or children. When that is the case, the non-custodial parent will likely be responsible for paying child support to help cover the expenses needed for the child's needs, such as education. Other things such as gifts, clothing or transportation are not considered part of the child support payment. Child support is usually based on the combined gross parental income, as follows:

- For one child: 17% of the combined parental income
- For two children: 25% of the combined parental income
- For three children: 29% of the combined parental income
- For four children: 31% of the combined parental income
- For five or more children: No less than 35% of the combined parental income

In some cases, a Judge may order the non-custodial parent to pay a share of the child or children's health care expenses, child care expenses, or education expenses, above and beyond basic child support. When a non-custodial parent does not meet their legal child support obligations, wage garnishments, property liens or income execution may be instituted through a court order or judgment. When a child reaches the age of 21 or is legally emancipated at an earlier age, child support will stop.

It is the responsibility of the custodial parent to track and keep a record of all child support payments so that documentation can be provided in the event of a dispute. Those parents who have joint physical custody of their children are required to inform the other parent if they intend to travel or leave the state with the children. Finally, another responsibility to keep in mind is the financial obligations that each custodial parent owes their children.

CONCLUSION

SUMMARY

By now you should be aware that it is integral to enter the custody process with a concise and clear plan. Winning your child custody battle comes down to a few key factors - meticulous preparation, credible and reliable witness, and a solid support system. Your focus should be on winning over the psychologist and Judge involved in your case by presenting yourself and your evidence clearly and accurately. Remember, whenever possible act out of logic over emotion and try to consistently showcase your best parenting skills.

The outcome of a child custody case differs greatly based on each situation, as there are countless aspects that come into play when determining the best place for a child to be raised. It is our hope that the strategies outlined in this book will help you avoid common mistakes and prepare your evidence effectively. By reading this guide, you are now significantly more prepared than you were prior to knowing this information. All the best to you and your family, from everyone at Brian D. Perskin & Associates P.C.

WE CAN HELP

Brian D. Perskin & Associates P.C. is one of the most trusted names in New York when it comes to divorce and child custody. Brian and his experienced team have earned a reputation as an aggressive, intelligent and strategic firm dedicated to their client's precise needs. The attorneys at Brian D. Perskin & Associates P.C. employ a dynamic team of experts to help protect their clients' interests and assets. These include forensic accountants to ensure no assets remain hidden by their spouses. Support personnel ensures their personal support needs – and those of their children – are always protected.

Don't take it from us; the following pages contain just a few examples of what our past clients have had to say about their experience working with us.

SUCCESS STORIES

"EXCELLENT AND POWERFUL REPRESENTATION"

Brian and his team are outstanding! Brian is a smart aggressive strategist and truly cares for his clients he immediately recognized my husbands personality issues and knew how to use this to our advantage he is clearly familiar with personality disorders and he used terms that only make sense for insiders who have dealt with manipulative aggressive people with power and control issues. I was also able to get primary parenting for my kids and a favorable property settlement. In court Brian was very concise and very powerful with his words leaving no stone unturned. Brian represented me in a very complicated divorce case in which business property and children were involved he is a smart and compassionate attorney who knows his stuff he was always available on the phone/email and responded to my inquires promptly. It was reassuring to know that this firm took my predicament seriously and took every effort to resolve what had been a long ordeal. With Brian's representation I was able to separate myself from years of legal harassment.

My husband at the time had opposing counsels employ unethical tactics to try and make me give up including dragging the case on and on. I never felt uninformed or unaware of the next steps or potential hang ups. I had found the perfect balance between a knowledgeable professional and a real person who understood how devastating and life changing it can be. Brian is definitely someone you want on your side I am very happy with my settlement and have exceeded my expectations I highly recommend using this firm for your divorce case.

"COULDN'T HAVE ASKED FOR A BETTER ATTORNEY"

From the moment I contacted Mr. Perskin's office, I knew I had found the right attorney. I was very stressed/overwhelmed by the whole divorce process. The process with Mr. Perskin went smoothly, I was always updated and everything turned out exactly as he explained. So on my "anniversary" I received the best gift ever; an e-mail from Mr. Perskins attaching the final divorce judgment! Thank you very much Mr. Perskin for your professionalism, hard work and for making my divorce process quick, easy and much less stressful. I will recommend him to friends and family who feel "left in the dark" and with few options, just like I did.

"QUICK, EASY AND STRAIGHTFORWARD"

Mr. Perskin is not only well-knowledged, straight-forward and professional, but he's also very pleasant to speak and interact with.

That may not be someone's top priority when searching for a family law attorney, but when having to discuss sensitive issues in detail, it makes a big difference. He certainly made the process as quick and painless as possible. In our first meeting, he clearly described what my options were and gave his suggestions and a time-frame. In the end, everything worked out to exactly how he said it would. Also, he's very responsive to status requests, so I never felt in the dark. Whatever your circumstance, if you need a family lawyer, look no further. Mr. Perskin is a get-it-done guy.

From Brian:

Thank you for reading
How to Win Child Custody
You can call me any time at 718 875-7584
Email me at bdp@perskinlaw.com
Visit my website: www.newyorkdivorceattorney.com
Schedule a consultation: https://live.vcita.com/site/brianperskin

LIST OF COUNTY CLERK'S OFFICES

New York City Counties:

Bronx County
851 Grand Concourse, Room 118
Bronx, New York 10451
866-797-7214

Kings County (Brooklyn)
360 Adams Street, Room 189
Brooklyn, New York 11201
347-404-9772

New York County (Manhattan)
60 Centre Street, Room 141B
New York, New York 10007
646-386-5955

Queens County
88-11 Sutphin Boulevard
Jamaica, New York 11435
718-298-0600

Richmond County (Staten Island)
130 Stuyvesant Place, 2nd Floor
Staten Island, New York 10301
718-675-7700

New York State Counties:

Albany County
16 Eagle Street, Room 128
Albany, New York 12207
518-487-5100

Allegany County
7 Court Street, Room 18
Belmont, New York 14813
585-268-9270

Broome County
60 Hawley Street
PO Box 2062
Binghamton, New York 13902
607-778-2255

Cattaraugus County
330 Court Street
Little Valley, New York 14755
716-938-2297

Cayuga County
160 Genesee Street, 1st Floor
Auburn, New York 13021
315-253-1271

Chautauqua County
1 North Erie Street
PO Box 170
Mayville, New York 14757
716-753-4331

Chemung County
210 Lake Street
Elmira, New York 14901
607-737-2920

Chenango County
5 Court Street
Norwich, New York 13815
607-337-1450

Clinton County
137 Margaret Street, 1st Floor
Plattsburgh, New York 12901
518-565-4700

Columbia County
560 Warren Street
Hudson, New York 12534
518-828-3339

Cortland County
46 Greenbush Street, Suite 105
Cortland, New York 13045
607-753-5021

Delaware County
Court House Square
PO Box 426
Delhi, New York 13753
607-746-2123

Dutchess County
22 Market Street
Poughkeepsie, New York 12601
845-486-2120

Erie County
92 Franklin Street
Buffalo, New York 14202
716-858-8785

Essex County
7559 Court Street
Elizabethtown, New York 12932
518-873-3600

Franklin County
355 West Main Street, Suite 248
PO Box 70
Malone, New York 12953
518-481-1681

Fulton County
223 West Main Street
Johnstown, New York 12095
518-736-5555

Genesee County
15 Main Street
Batavia, New York 14020
858-344-2550, ext 2243

Greene County
411 Main Street
Catskill, New York 12414
518-719-3255

Hamilton County
Courthouse
PO Box 204 Route 8
Lake Pleasant, New York 12108
518-548-7111

Herkimer County
109 Mary Street, Suite 1111
Herkimer, New York 13350
315-867-1129

Jefferson County
175 Arsenal Street
Watertown, New York 13601
315-785-3081

Lewis County
7660 State Street
Lowville, New York 13367
315-376-5333

Livingston County
6 Court Street, Room 201
Geneseo, New York 14454
585-243-7010

Madison County
138 North Court Street
PO Box 668
Wampsville, New York 13163
315-366-2261

Monroe County
101 County Clerk's Office Building
39 West Maine Street
Rochester, New York 14614
585-753-1600

Montgomery County
64 Broadway
PO Box 1500
Fonda, New York 12068
518-853-8111

Nassau County
240 Old County Road
Mineola, New York 11501
516-571-2664

Niagara County
175 Hawley Street
PO Box 4561
Lockport, New York 14094
716-439-7022

Oneida County
800 Park Avenue
Utica, New York 13501
315-798-5794

Onondaga County
401 Montgomery Street, Room 200
Syracuse, New York 13202
315-435-2227

Ontario County
20 Ontario Street
Canandaigua, New York 14424
585-396-4200

Orange County
Parry Building
4 Glenmere Cove Road
Goshen, New York 10924
845-291-2690

Orleans County
3 South Main Street
Albion, New York 14411
585-589-5334

Oswego County
46 East Bridge Street
Oswego, New York 13120
315-349-8385

Otsego County
197 Main Street
PO Box 710
Cooperstown, New York 13326
607-574-4276

Putnam County
40 Gleneida Avenue
Carmel, New York 10512
845-225-3641, ext 300

Rensselaer County
105 Third Street
Troy, New York 12180
518-270-4080

Rockland County
1 South Main Street, Suite 100
New City, New York 10956
845-638-5070

Saratoga County
40 McMaster Street
Ballston Spa, New York 12020
518-885-2213

Schenectady County
620 State Street, 3rd Floor
Schenectady, New York 12305
518-388-4225

Schoharie County
PO Box 549
Schoharie, New York 12157
518-295-8316

Schuyler County
105 Ninth Street, Unit 8
Watkins Glen, New York 14891
607-535-8133

Seneca County
1 DiPronio Drive
Waterloo, New York 13165
315-539-1771

Saint Lawrence County
Building #2
48 Court Street
Canton, New York 13617
315-379-2237

Steuben County
3 East Pulteney Square
Bath, New York 14810
607-776-9631

Suffolk County
310 Center Drive
Riverhead, New York 11901
631-852-2000

Sullivan County
100 North Street
PO Box 5012
Monticello, New York 12701
845-807-0411

Tioga County
16 Court Street
PO Box 307
Owego, New York 13827
607-687-8660

Tompkins County
320 North Tioga Street
Ithaca, New York 14850
607-274-5431

Ulster County
244 Fair Street
PO Box 1800
Kingston, New York 12401
845-340-3000

Warren County
1340 State Route 9
Lake George, New York 12845
518-761-6429

Washington County
Municipal Center, Building A
393 Broadway
Fort Edward, New York 12828
518-746-2170

Wayne County
9 Pearl Street
PO Box 608
Lyons, New York 14489
315-946-7470

Westchester County
110 Dr. Martin Luther King Jr. Boulevard
White Plains, New York 10601
914-995-3080

Wyoming County
143 North Main Street, Suite 104
Warsaw, New York 14569
585-786-8810

Yates County
417 Liberty Street, Suite 1107
Penn Yan, New York 14527
315-536-5120

Printed in the United States
By Bookmasters